The Wounds of Faith

Twelve Decades of Sonnets

Michael Robinson

THE WOUNDS OF FAITH

© 2023 Michael Robinson. All rights reserved. No part of this book may be copied, reproduced or transmitted by any means without prior permission of the author, except in the case of brief quotations embodied in review articles.

Cataloguing-in-Publication entry is available from the National Library of Australia http:/catalogue.nla.gov.au/.

This edition first published in Hackham, South Australia by Immortalise via Ingram Spark in November 2023
www.immortalise.com.au

ISBN paperback 978-0-6457721-7-3
       ebook   978-0-6457721-6-6

Typesetting and cover by Ben Morton

The Wounds of Faith

Twelve Decades of Sonnets

Michael Robinson

Acknowledgements

Poems in this collection have appeared in the following print and on-line journals:
Catholic Poetry Room, *ChristArt*, *Oxygen*, *Poetry Matters*, *Poetry for Public Transport*, *Studio*.

Preparation of this collection was supported by a grant from the Western Australian Department of Local Government, Sport and Cultural Industries.

Department of
Local Government, Sport and Cultural Industries
GOVERNMENT OF WESTERN AUSTRALIA

Contents

Acknowledgements..iv
Preface..1

I. The Wounds of Faith

The Lake..9
The Valley..10
Hollow Moon...11
Present Winds..12
Secret Harmonies...13
The Wounds of Faith...14
After Rain..15
Mountains of Evening..16
The Sky's Command..17
Flutes..18

II. The Trembling Path

The Sleeping Range...21
The Trembling Path...22
The Fallen Day...23
The Violin..24
Vestiges of Days...25
The Broken Summit...26
The Wind's Whispers...27
The Heartless Winds..28
Ended by Fire...29
Intercession...30

III. The Gathering Sky

The Lost..33
The Maze...34
Recollection...35
Secrecies...36
Nothing Is Hidden...37

That Barren Might..38
The Sea..39
The Sniper..40
Silver Sea..41
The Gathering Sky..42

IV. The Broken Shield

The Broken Shield..45
What The Night Has Made..46
Traces of War...47
The Table..48
Autumns of Injury..49
Visions of Freedom..50
The Waterfall...51
The Light..52
The Walls...53
The Bloodstained and the Good..54

V. The Burning Bowl

Fields of Night...57
Immediate Thunder..58
Rivers of Night..59
The Burning Bowl..60
The Mind..61
The Life-Raft...62
The Droplet and the Sea..63
Air from Heaven..64
The Mourner..65
The Thief..66

VI. The Mounting Tide

Faith...69
The Choice...70
Gate of Emptiness..71
Hours of Emptiness..72

The Bridge..73
Spirit's Dawning...74
Forgotten Hills...75
The Mounting Tide..76
The Moonflower..77
The Vow...78

VII. A Vine Dances

Hades...81
The Waking Stars..82
A Vine Dances..83
The Hidden Rose...84
The Library...85
Mind's Fire..86
The Rose...87
The Scales...88
Tides of Daybreak...89
The Fountain...90

VIII. Sanctities of Dawn

The Shivering Flame...93
Orchards..94
Seeds of Kindness...95
Dawn...96
Shadows of Ecstasy...97
Sanctities of Dawn..98
Mists...99
The Land Set Free..100
The Cliff...101
Faithful Joy..102

IX. Immortalities

Immortalities..105
King of Fire..106
Silences..107

Calming the Tides..108
The Fleeting Land..109
The Mirror and the Tree..110
The Sighs of Time...111
The Window..112
The Sun Awakes...113
The Sea's Amazement..114

X. Gatherer of Days

Absolution..117
Gatherer of Days...118
Cloud of Mystery...119
The Sculptor..120
Islands...121
Moments of Light..122
The Day...123
Before the Sun..124
Marigolds...125
Miracles...126

XI. The Feather

The Song...129
Hand of God..130
The Veil...131
Love and Symmetry..132
Havens..133
The Comet..134
Artisan...135
The Glade...136
The Golden Cave..137
The Feather..138

XII. The Sleeping Sea

The Flame...141
The Sleeping Sea...142

Night Sky..143
The Coast..144
Above the Cliff...145
The Comforter...146
Love's Logic..147
Ruined Beginnings..148
The Child...149
The Stray Bird...150

Preface

"Poetry may be considered to be the gift of moving the affections through the imagination, and its object to be the beautiful." John Henry Newman (*Essays Critical and Historical*, I, 29) offers this as a corrective, or rather a supplement, to his earlier remark that for Christians (and, we may feel, for others also), "a poetical view of things is a duty. We are bid to colour all things with hues of faith, to see a divine meaning in every event" (I, 23).

Poetry is an art; and it is an art that involves a way of seeing. Newman's first observation focuses on the poet's vision, the way in which he or she should view God, the world and his or her fellow beings; his second, on the purpose and orientation of the art of poetry, which is to move the reader. One may have a poetical view of things without being a poet oneself; many people do. Ideally all, whether poets or not, should; but a poet without a poetical view of things will be in a grim case indeed.

It would be easy to think of the first, the poet's vision, as the more important. Of course, if we are to practise the art of poetry, whether as readers or writers, the reader's response to poetry is equally important. And it should be emphasised that in Newman's argument the colours and the divine meaning of which he speaks are not projected by the human consciousness but are really there. Consequently, they can be rightly or wrongly perceived, rightly or wrongly expressed. And the link with poetry as the gift of moving the affections through the imagination is evident: the imagination must work on things as they are.

How then can poetry's object be the beautiful? And how can it approach its object? Not all things are beautiful; some are ugly, some are deeply distressing. One cannot, or at any rate need not, select only the pleasant and graceful as subject matter. And it is obviously tempting to approach unattractive subject matter by writing in unattractive ways. But a just evocation of the ugly will at some point contrast it with beauty. This may be an explicit contrast, or it may be implicit in the quality of the writing. One way or another, if the art is good art, the contrast will be there.

An adequate portrayal of a damaged, sinful, even wicked human person will reveal something of the unique human dignity of every human person; it will thereby demonstrate the tragedy of human failure, suffering and sin. And in this way it will show, if only by implication, that there are or were different possibilities. If there is no choice, no moments of decision, there is neither tragedy, satire nor comedy.

Poetry requires both perceptions as accurate as can be managed and the materials to portray them. To have an awareness of a scene, a situation, a person, is one thing; to make – to attempt to make – a work of art from it is another; and the two are likely to react one upon the other. Skill, in writing or reading or both, needs finely tuned awareness and is likely to contribute to its growth.

The practice of art, like the practice of philosophy, science (which is not limited to the physical sciences) or theology, requires that there be truth independent of our thoughts and interpretations, even though we can never fully reach it or do it justice, whether in art or another field. And truth is not to be reduced to the study of any one aspect of things. If a table is said to be a multiplicity of atoms swirling around in a void, that is only to say that, if looked at in a certain way, it will appear so. Looked at in another way, it is a table.

It isn't possible for the human intellect to perceive things in all their different facets. But that does not mean that we can't perceive them at all, or that truth is a matter of one's personal "perspective."

We see realities, though imperfectly. We see nature in its myriad facets. And we see – though, again, never completely – our living, suffering, growing or dwindling fellow human beings. All this is necessary for art, philosophy and theology, and the physical and other sciences.

Like many people, I have seen death and suffering close at hand. These matters are among the subjects of the poems in this collection. And when we see these things, we do not see merely behaviour, as a past school of psychologists pretended. Nor do we construct or conjecture them from "sense data," as positivist and empiricist philosophers have argued. Still less, when we perceive our fellow human beings *in extremis*, or for that matter in joy, do we see representatives of one or another identity group; we encounter living individuals. I have learned, or had it reinforced, through working with homeless people, former prisoners and others, that human dignity transcends the classes, races, genders, sexualities and politics by which too many would divide us.

We may be approaching the end of a period in which poets have felt that their art required them to pursue the casual, the vernacular, the cynical, even the incoherent. The casual and the vernacular undeniably have their place, but should never become requirements to the exclusion of other styles. If they become orthodoxies, they can be as stifling as eighteenth-century neoclassicism is often (though not entirely accurately) thought to have been. The cynical and the incoherent, when cultivated, not in the context of a larger view, but as alternatives to grace, order and form, can become deathly.

Painters and sculptors, with some honourable exceptions, have preferred the tangled, the irrational, the disordered; architects have worked towards the merely functional and the brutal. These, like all fashions, will change. In the meantime, it would be tempting to trim one's sails to the prevailing wind. But this would lead to a Sargasso Sea of conformity; and would run counter to the call to try to do justice to any aspect of reality – even to a Sargasso Sea, which, though rich with life, and fascinating in its way, is distinct from the greater ocean, and can only be understood in relation to it.

Poetry aims to evoke, to reveal the true and the beautiful. It cannot do this completely and all at once. But it can endeavour to be as truthful, and as beautiful, as it can, given the limited scope that is part of its being.

To try to evoke realities truthfully in any art means that we must at the same time strive for beauty. (Naturally I don't claim to have succeeded in either.) It is a remarkable truth that truthfulness and beauty are not incompatible; quite the opposite; they require one another. Truthfulness requires form and grace; in literature, including poetry, it requires respect for language, its meanings, its sounds, its history, its rhythms. And so does beauty.

Both beauty and truthfulness in art must come with skill, craft, formal coherence. The sonnet (of which the poems in this book follow a slightly unorthodox pattern) is an instance, among many, of a form that enables and encourages the evocation of truths.

The themes of this book are grief, trauma and recovery; faith and its wounds – the wounds faith must suffer and the wounds that will be endured if one tries to live in faith; faith and its joy. As there is a connection between compassion and suffering, so there is a connection between these two, on the one hand, and thought, language, art and faith on the other.

The world as it is requires us to care for one another, sometimes at the cost of sacrifice; to care for nature; to try (as difficult as it is) to think clearly; and to respect language and art. These – and first of all compassion – are among the summonings of faith. "If I have all faith, so as to remove mountains, but do not have love, I am nothing" (I Corinthians 13:2). And, as it has seemed to me and to others, the call to love, compassion and truth illuminates the possibility and the source of faith.

As Newman reminds us, a poetical view of things is a duty, one that requires us to see the meaning in things, not limited to but including human persons, and in events. And if it is a duty, it is also a source of delight. For an artist joy is a duty, and duty is a joy. Poetry is the attempt to move the heart and the imagination by portraying things with the meaning that, though we often miss it, is integral to them, using language with whatever skill and humility we can bring to the task. If joy is shared with a reader, the work is achieved.

The Wounds of Faith

I. The Wounds of Faith

The Wounds of Faith

The Lake

I have died not once but many days
Without hospital bed or pain relief,
Endured alone the tyranny of brief
Or year-long, decades-long illness, the haze
Of symptoms and of surgery that weighs
On body, spirit, mind. Then time, the thief
Of history and hope and old belief
Leaves houses ruined. Nonetheless I praise
The maker of the rain and galaxies
That I have woken fresh from slow unease
And past collapse, attentions of the knife
And scalpel, for the offer of new life,
And for a lake that glimmered under cloud
When evening fell and hills and valleys bowed.

The Valley

Long instants of eternity will light
The strident valley and its suffering,
So that the matted, muddled soul must sing
And dance under the slanting weather's blight,
Cold hailstones' massed weight, and may rest, despite
Downpours of winter and the thundering
That scatters farms and brings floods gathering,
May know the peace that steers the white bird's flight.
Bare, hungry, thoughtless creature that I am,
Bedraggled sheep or stray, bewildered lamb,
Fit only for the slaughterhouse, and yet
Time out of time shall lift me from the wet
Fields and sodden pastures and shall mend
The muddy paddocks and the forest's end.

Hollow Moon

What thing is this that fades, falters, contrives
To wake in darkness, drowse and dream in light,
Groping for comprehension and insight,
Bewildered by its grieving? What survives
Of all its rough, impassioned, heedless lives
In train or office, warm bed of delight,
The brutal years of solitude and flight?
I stroll the riverbanks when spring arrives,
Observe the quick yachts racing on cool streams,
The distant blazing of a house that gleams,
Grey, settled hills and shattered rocks that rise,
And find eternity before these eyes,
Watching the gardens and an afternoon,
The tranquil sun, the half-seen, hollow moon.

Present Winds

The landscape lifts its gaze and spreads its wings.
A radiance of grass flows through white cloud.
Each low hill, fence and mountain chants aloud
And every passing rock rises and sings
Melodies encompassing all things,
Gentler than early morning. Earth, be proud,
For now your kind creator has endowed
Your battle-hardened years with light that brings
Music transcending hours, and floods the free,
Victorious gulfs of time with symmetry,
With flowers to transcend the dawn's crisp dew,
Stony ascents and old paths always new,
Play of the soul answering to the call
Of present winds and seeds that fly and fall.

Secret Harmonies

Stars tremble and flutter in the supreme
Emptiness of evening. The grey lake spreads
Opaque, smooth ripples. Low hills bow their heads,
Murmur their silent music to a stream
Of breaking, faint patterns of light that gleam
On water, bushes, earth and thin reeds' beds.
A line of wind comes from the north and sheds
Voices over the living night. They seem
To gather in their calmness years that flow,
Storms that have come and passed decades ago,
Forgotten crimes that haunt the centuries,
Long hidden souls and secret harmonies.
The lake recedes into remote shadows,
Quiet, urgent whispers and soft echoes.

The Wounds of Faith

The slow drug draws her tangled, knotted head
To drowse on a tawdry metal table.
Her small boy beside her, inscrutable,
Watches with uncomprehending dread.
A young man, scarred, barefooted, finds his bed
Under night shadows, cold, invisible.
No soul that lives is irredeemable.
Faith walks among the grieving and the dead.
These are the wounds of faith. It will not slight
The shattered and rejected, though it might
(How easy that would be), nor turn aside
From its own guilt in arrogance and pride,
Endures the blades of truth in love and fear,
And knows, when blood returns, that God is near.

After Rain

A river spreads, foams, rushes after rain
That veiled forests and pastures in dense grey
Curtains that soared and swirled, faded away
To cold, thick drops. Green banks fight to contain
Hurried waters that bear the shifting stain
Of light fallen from broken clouds to stray
Over young, ephemeral tides that play,
And puzzle an observer to explain
How stream, current, paddock and storm can be
Unique in all their multiplicity.
The song of the wind floods over the grassed
Fields, raw spinneys, laments all that is past
And future, harmonises death and sky,
And in that chant high trees delight and sigh.

Mountains of Evening

The spirit peeps out from the frail body's
Changing, shifting currents of salt and sand,
Calls out (but half unheard) a soft command,
Or lamentations, imprecations, pleas,
Responds, or half responds, to melodies
Drifting between cold waters and warm land,
Or echoes gulls' faint cries. It cannot stand,
Divided from its flesh in long unease,
And returns to the deathly life of stone
And grass, alive to wind and air alone,
Or to the slow ache of cattle, when rain
Caresses green paddocks. It wakes to pain,
Looks through the veil of twilight at the steep
Mountains of evening; sinks back into sleep.

The Sky's Command

Cool, flat plains of sand stretch to the furthest
Limits of ocean where the placid shore
Meets the wide, sleeping, dreaming river's more
Than worldly calm. Pain compounds interest
As bitter test succeeds on bitter test
And adds new burdens to the rising store,
Balance of day's betrayal, midnight's war,
I carry to this beach. Then what is best?
Never to have been born or to be where
The leaping birds play in the salty air
Above the river's mouth, take sudden flight,
Tiny creatures eddy in pools of light
And water, strings of seaweed tend the sand,
Slapping wavelets cherish the sky's command?

Flutes

Flutes question me with tender notes that sway.
Warm, hollow breath and subtle melodies
Call back to mind relinquished memories,
Abandoned thoughts and hopes long thrown away.
Soft lips and tongues and hidden fingers play
On silver instruments with golden keys
Elaborate entwining harmonies,
Perplexing visions of a vanished day.
Theirs is the music from beyond the world,
The cool, haunting orchestrations unfurled,
Fluttering in the deep valleys of night,
Old sorrows and reproaches lost to sight,
Slow elegies for unremembered wrong,
The secret summons of the murmured song.

II. The Trembling Path

The Wounds of Faith

The Sleeping Range

A grey hawk's wings beat the hard air and call
Fresh winds to gust around a mountain's crest.
Leaves, twigs and soft feathers compose its nest
In a stony cleft above a fierce wall
Of impenetrable rock, a craggy fall
To sand. It bears the heart of a distressed
Young soldier, torn still beating from his breast,
Places it with new eggs, old bones and all
Its avian treasures. The heart pulses, gleams,
Dark, red, mottled, weighted with loves and dreams.
When twilight comes and peaks and ravines fade,
It pours scarlet rays into growing shade,
Illuminates moss with crimson. Slow, strange,
Impassive blood crosses the sleeping range.

The Trembling Path

The sun drops into dark and cold ocean
That slaps and chops in rolling restlessness.
What falls below the surface none can guess,
Small lives gliding, black and white striped, stolen
Creatures, tendrils floating, hard eyes, poison,
Seaweed, uncountable currents, blindness,
Immeasurable dying, fruitfulness.
As the round sun spreads on the horizon,
It casts a golden road across the sea
That ripples, breaks, returns, meets the jetty,
Ragged and windworn, reaching from the sand
Out into the comfortless waves. I stand
On grey, bleak, weathered, rough wood and survey
The jewelled, trembling path, the close of day.

The Fallen Day

When all the world is a harmonious night,
Songs and violin music pass from peaks
To gullies, cliffs to plains, and rhythm speaks
Legends of passion, thoughts and loves that might
Live on forever in the fires' despite.
Black-winged eagles carrying months and weeks
And hours like banners streaming from stern beaks
Hold in sharp claws the moon's and sun's last light,
Fluttering, fading. Those great eagles fly
Westward into the drowning of the sky
In seas of darkness and the memory
Of hills' and harvests' green tranquillity.
A new star rises from clouds' choral, grey
Funeral dirges for the fallen day.

The Violin

Invincible, ephemeral and strange,
Moments pour from empty mountains and roll
Into the years' abyss none may control,
Caverns of endless death no thought can change,
Historian nor vandal disarrange.
Cascading instants constitute the whole
Adventure of the flesh and house the soul
With all its hunger. The threatening range
Of peaks and ice and craggy gullies waits,
Impervious to pleadings or debates,
Allows the piercing violin its sweet
And flowing melody, supreme, complete,
Mounted in shadowed harmonies and long
Textures of stillness, plenitudes of song.

Vestiges of Days

Black and pitted with greens and varied greys,
The sea swells and coruscates in the light
From a single star that governs the night
And banishes the vestiges of days,
Drives away constellations. Its rays
Touch with sharp flame the cold waves' leaping height,
Reach down to changing currents' glide and flight,
Pattern the dark horizon with displays
Of fire from west and south to north and east.
A rock lifts flooding shoulders like a beast
Summoned from its ancestral ocean fold
To founder in high waters flecked with gold.
Seaweed in clumps and strands trails down steep sides,
Fades into silver foam and spreading tides.

The Broken Summit

Lightning explodes above a stony peak,
Illuminating rough rock streaked with snow
And trees that suffer on the slopes below
The broken summit. Curtains of rain wreak
Unanswerable vengeance on the meek
And uncomplaining leaves that blaze and glow
In sudden leaping rifts and undergo
Transformation into brilliant, sleek,
Fugitive bells of flame. A dancer springs
And whirls, twists, wanders, pirouettes and wings
Invisibly, vividly through the storm,
Wrapped in her grace and rhythm, art and form,
Clothed in cool sheets of fire that wend, flow, turn
Immeasurable clouds to cliffs that burn.

The Wind's Whispers

I wandered a descent bright with rivers,
Nodding, sighing flowers, white and golden,
Trunks reaching from the rich, secret, riven
Earth into soft air and the wind's whispers,
Growing with joy. Pale and moss-patched boulders
Absorbed the sun. I saw, partly hidden
In long reeds, a living body fallen,
Hefted it and bore it on my shoulders.
It was my sullied self. Under the load
Of present, past and future cares, I strode
Cautiously forward, burdened by the weight
That was my beaten, bloodied life, so late
Acknowledged. Crows and ravens in high trees
Cried out their anger and their long unease.

The Heartless Winds

A day will break when murdered souls will rise,
After nights, mornings, months and centuries,
Tomorrow or when all the symmetries
Of history shall cast off their disguise,
Conclude, and the last ash fall from the skies.
They will come from wells, fields and cities,
Take up renewed and healed, mended bodies
And look the lost who killed them in their eyes,
Requiring years and lifetimes at their hands,
Countries not explored and relinquished lands.
Bereaved lovers, children, parents will groan
Once more, lamenting seas and shores unknown.
They will forgive, when stars dwindle and fade,
The heartless winds, the gesture of a blade.

Ended by Fire

No murder is accomplished in a void,
And not only the dead are lost. A gun
Resounds in clean, soft air. A child, undone
By terror, sees a man collapse, destroyed,
Ended by fire no spirit can avoid,
Amazed, dishonoured. Imminent prison
Wounds the guilty and his guiltless children,
Their world, the years they once could have enjoyed,
Removed by a hard law. And others mourn
A rough provider who will not return,
Who loved them though he could not always pay
Accounts, who fell one afternoon and lay
On helpless earth as if immersed in deep,
Mythological dreams or tranquil sleep.

Intercession

Tonight and in your kindness every day
Remember in your prayers those who suffer
From human savagery in peace or war,
All those who flinch when hatred starts to play
In helpless eyes or blind passions betray,
Doctor, surgeon, nurse, police officer,
All who greet with care the maimed survivor,
And let none scorn the work of those who pray.
The streets grow murderous, and fools explode
In righteousness, and cruelty stalks the road.
The innocent wake to nightmare and bleed,
The blood-soaked guilty laugh and work and feed.
Pray also for the lost who walk forlorn
Paths of violence, and for their children.

III. The Gathering Sky

The Wounds of Faith

The Lost

Beside the blank road streaming in the heat,
Between still fields and ageing bitumen,
Cars at intervals lie waiting, broken,
Burning in their temporary defeat
Or fading into rust, their end complete,
Scorned like families destroyed, like children
Abandoned by their age, future stolen,
Home shattered, left to founder in the street.
Here a shredded tyre, a semi-trailer
Angled, overturned, spilt on the shoulder,
Dull paint glowing, disconsolate, to be
Salvaged by lumbering machinery,
Cranes, winches. Who then shall redeem the lost
From paths mad, savage history has crossed?

The Maze

I have known friends who died when time was due,
Men and women, antique and full of days.
They saw fresh morning light, soft evening rays,
Had done much that the world had asked them, knew
Their hours approached an end. Their spirits flew
Willingly to assist the choirs of praise,
Dismissed now from the madness and the maze
Of death and history to live anew.
But when a child is taken all must mourn,
A father murdered, children left forlorn,
A woman made to give up her scarred soul,
Poisoned, never comforted, never whole,
Summoned untimely from the newborn rose,
The flax's green, sharp blades, young vine that glows.

Recollection

"*Non. Je ne regrette rien.*" How can that be?
How can you live under the winds of day,
Never endure past errors come to flay
Coasts, shorelines of contentment? As for me,
Should I venture rashly onto the sea
Of recollection, rips pull, cold sharks prey,
Reefs, rocks, whirlpools, waterspouts threaten. Grey,
Rainy mists obscure the slow tragedy
Of disappeared sailors. Predatory teeth
Discard shy, wayward, fractured bones beneath
Uncountable currents. Only the drowned,
No, not even the drowned forget. Profound
Mercy glows above deep clouds. None but God
Redeems the breaking tides, waves Christ once trod.

Secrecies

They move towards me, souls alive with peace,
Absorbed in daily tasks of work and rest,
Harried by children, shopping, or oppressed
By business, showing marks of love or ease,
Unquenchable desire to help and please.
But there is one, not spoken, unconfessed,
Who carries deep within a mundane breast
Rage without end, cherishes memories
Of murder, torment, shame; plans, walking past,
Some cruelty still darker than his last,
Or hers. No mark reveals it to the day.
She will not ask for pardon, fall what may,
Or he. None knows who. Nor who hesitates
Before the pitch of crime that desolates.

Nothing Is Hidden

Nothing is hidden. All must be revealed.
Incursions of the ants; a tree's grey trunk
Termites excavate. Libraries have sunk
Beneath earth's waves. A soldier dropped his shield,
Five thousand years ago, where paddocks yield
Barley and rye. A meditative monk
Laboured and prayed with others who had drunk
Waters of contemplation unconcealed,
Open to all who feel the sun and hear
The first rain at the turning of the year.
The murderer who cowered from the gaze
Of truth shall tremble at the end of days.
The victim fallen on cold ground and dew
Shall wake and touch white roses, fresh bamboo.

That Barren Might

Clatter of gunfire patterns vacant night.
Small explosions perforate grey, soft air,
Echoes of hate, aggression and despair.
Cars glide around corners, loaded with spite
And mean, cramped minds whose lonely thoughts take flight,
Crack doorframes and glass panes beyond repair,
Send messages of agony that tear
Bodies, break hearts and bones. War's barren might,
Coward's courage maims the dull, bloodstained sky.
Old injuries and grudges multiply.
Past feuds begun bleak centuries ago,
For worlds long dead, renew themselves and show
Time's breath kills. Nor shall any carry guilt
But for the blood their living hands have spilt.

The Sea

Glimmering, foaming, open to the sun,
Ocean endures its hidden depths of cold.
Scarlet, green, black, sunken wars, never told,
Armies of rushing, changing waves that run,
Gather around reefs; battles never done,
Peace never made. The sea itself grows old,
And I remember all that thought can hold
Of suffering and murder once begun,
Continued always while the breakers roar
And flood, and spread white froth along the shore,
And leave their fading patterns on pale sand.
Trails of seaweed and spray parch on the strand.
The barren heat of past centuries glows
On dunes and stones, and where the warm wind blows.

The Sniper

What place can be found on this tormented
Earth's unquiet surface that has not known
Inhuman human cruelty, or flown
Scarlet flags of violence, lamented
Love discarded, murder unrepented?
Graves of orchids, highways, gardens of stone,
Land sloping to a far valley, a lone
Sniper's gunshot, mercy circumvented.
What mountain range or city could give calm?
What old and fertile jungle, what young farm?
Maybe the frozen peaks of jagged white
That soar above the harsh Antarctic night,
Inhospitable always to warm minds,
Serene and fierce among the prowling winds.

Silver Sea

Walk around the bodies on the roadside
Huddled in bright blankets or wreathed in poor,
Threadbare jackets. Tread softly and ignore
The ruin of civilisation's pride,
The crumbling stone, empty windows and wide
Gaps between bricks where winds whistle and pour.
Lies whisper endless messages of war.
Parents mourn sons and daughters who have died.
King Priam lost heirs to fierce Achilles,
These to despair and poverty's unease,
Inconsequent gangs, cheap drugs that destroy.
Outside the looming walls of stately Troy,
A soldier fell to his last agony,
Remembering white sails and silver sea.

The Gathering Sky

A man condemned and fastened to time's wheel,
Dying under his life's history's blows,
Finds how the sky gathers itself and shows
Glory on glory. Opening clouds reveal
Angels robed in white and crimson to heal
Martyrs of the centuries with pillows
Of gold satin and gentle song. Light grows,
More than the superseded sun, more real.
Doves and eagles lift their eternal wings
And glide into cold air that flows and sings
Over blue lakes and a forest that bears
Undying apples, hymns, oranges, prayers,
Ripe leaves and harmonies that shall not cease,
Rising mountains, timeless valleys of peace.

IV. The Broken Shield

The Wounds of Faith

The Broken Shield

I thought to turn away from violence,
The blows, deceits, brutalities that played
Like flames hurrying through bushland. I laid
Plans for healing, leisure and new patience,
Poetry and music, song and silence.
In restful gardens, offices' grey shade,
Minds can be damaged, spirits bruise and fade
Through sieges of the night. Then get you hence,
All you (if there are any such) who hold
That years can bring respite from griefs of old.
New sorrow still must come and still surprise
And teach the battered heart to empathise,
The blood-stained battle-axe, the broken shield,
The truth and glory passing wars revealed.

What The Night Has Made

Pains of the sharp-edged knife or razor's blade,
Torn skin and shining blood that wells and pours
And splashes on the grass; then moonlight draws
Attention to the brilliance and the shade,
The mystery of what the night has made,
Impassiveness of trees; or nature's laws
Compelling fierce, remorseless teeth and claws,
Or cracked and aching bones. These pangs must fade,
Fall into legend. Only the mind's grief
Stirs and endures through years with small relief,
Returns before dawn, vivid still to wake
The sleeping soul and bring the heart to break
And pulse to wander, though deep valleys play
Sweet songs of silent joy to herald day.

Traces of War

The flesh is weak and frail and cannot bear
The violence of bullets that invade
Its dark and secret organs, or the blade
Cutting through wool, cotton and skin to tear
Veins and let blood run loose. A stranger's glare,
Emerging out of shadows into shade,
Portends a newborn wound that will not fade
Though body mend. The soul's eternal air,
A breath of the divine that leaves the skies
And centuries, and looks through grieving eyes,
Intangible and undetectable,
Carries long memories of its battle
Though none can see them. New assailants draw
Insatiable defeat from changeless war.

The Table

Wade into a river of scalding flame,
Golden, yellow, crimson, burning below
Banks of red earth, brown rock, small hills that glow
Dully in the morning. Endure the name
Of a burns victim; clamber, limping, lame,
Out onto the far shore. Glance back and know
Always the brilliant, colourful fires flow
Westward to a blazing sea. Bear the shame
Of third-degree scars. Hobble onward, find,
Risen from the hot afternoon, behind
Low cliffs and blackened scrub, a welcoming
Mansion where unknown, dancing voices bring
Forgotten peace, warm music, a banquet,
Good company, roast meat, the table set.

Autumns of Injury

Nothing is more mysterious than this,
The selfhood of a dragonfly that whirrs,
Sudden uniqueness of a flight that blurs
When a bird leaves its covert, vanishes
Among high, ephemeral images.
And then the wonder of a soul that errs,
Fails, collapses, rises, that beauty stirs
And art restores, that loves and moves and is.
It has its life that nothing can replace,
No tyranny or argument deface.
It grows through memories and suffers long
Autumns of injury, winters of wrong.
Truth meets it on the winds of time and shows
Impassioned flesh the meaning of a rose.

Visions of Freedom

For thirty-seven years he felt the air,
In prison more than out, amid a daze
Of dull routine and injury, bare greys,
Drab greens, unending vigilance, the rare
Moments of kindness that are everywhere,
Even beyond the hardest walls that raise
Towers and walkways into morning haze,
Visions of freedom, living hours and care.
And then he died. The needle worked its ill.
He slept and dreamed slow dreams, lay cold and still.
And God who made him knows the dancing flame,
The melody he carried with his name
Above the sullen ache, the long unease,
And weeping angels sing his elegies.

The Waterfall

Upon what plain, what valley or what shore
Where cold, clear ripples play or high waves pound,
Red, rugged hill or floral, gentle mound
Where green leaves, golden petals, fine stems soar,
Beside what waterfall where sunbeams pour
And sparkle in the foam, what fertile ground,
Stony field ranges of iron surround,
Shall I now wander where the rising score
Of history, brutality and lust
Has not left human blood marking the dust,
Searing the water or the silver grass?
Hours move above the land, grey evenings pass
And deepen into night. Circlets of stars
Wake above darkened quarrels, endless wars.

The Light

Confronting once again the lately dead,
The visions of the many who have died
In sudden or protracted homicide,
From cancer or from words that were not said,
Gestures not given, tenderness that fled,
A woman lying crushed on the roadside,
Her shopping scattered, or a man who sighed,
Presented with the truth, and turned his head,
I learn again how lives are more than flight
Of random atoms in the silent light,
How each, despite the legions who would roll
The world in chaos, has its unquenched soul,
Held in eternity, remembered, named,
Imperishable, whole, though lost and maimed.

The Walls

Some set themselves to hide from death and build,
While years, months, decades fall past into deep,
Warm gulfs of irrecoverable sleep,
From stone and concrete, thought scattered, time spilled,
Walls and fortifications planned and willed
To hold the gales of grief at bay and keep
Tranquillity in granite. And some leap,
Faithful, when summoned, to the battlefield,
To face hard plains of sacrifice below
The swirling seasons and the rains that flow
From long forgotten oceans. They shall wake
And watch the light of heaven's morning break
Over the wreckage of the histories,
The changeless music and the living seas.

The Bloodstained and the Good

I lived with murder and confronted war
In its complex confusion and dismay,
Faced violence when others turned away.
I carried weaknesses and passed the door
To sufferings that worldly thoughts ignore,
Healed, or tried to, the wounded where they lay
In shining fields, on gravel or in grey
Apartments muffled by the city's roar,
A broken town, a ruined neighbourhood.
My colleagues were the bloodstained and the good,
Who went where only damaged souls may go,
Found compensations most decline to know,
An injured child who wandered in fine rain,
Rescued from death to comfort others' pain.

V. The Burning Bowl

The Wounds of Faith

Fields of Night

I lived calm days till the catastrophe,
The power and the vividness of white
Stars when they fell from burning fields of night
And flooded roads and towns with agony.
Then, waking from long sleep, it seemed to me,
Dismayed, I saw the moon and planets fight,
Searing the shops and streets with globes of light,
Rolling from shining parks into the sea,
So that strollers ran for their cars and fled
Before comets rushing from overhead,
Inescapable violence of ice,
Fire and snow; or in quiet suburbs' peace
Took shelter while roads, tents and cities died,
Endured visions of empty space that sighed.

Immediate Thunder

> Where France in all her towns lay vibrating
> Like some becalmed Bark beneath the burst
> Of Heaven's immediate Thunder
> — Coleridge, "To William Wordsworth," 29-31

Time has its madness and it weaves a cloud
That mounts in ambuscades above tired earth,
Draws poisoned waters from the seas of death.
And from that storm unerring lightnings, proud,
Sharp, fill the firmament, measured by loud,
Immediate thunder. And they strike at birth,
Divide the trusting infant's world, break truth
Into a thousand shining fragments, vowed,
Forgotten and abandoned. Once combined
Bodies and rich humanities, entwined,
Enabling new life, scatter, tear apart
The comfort of a young child's very heart,
Darken highway, town and city. They choke
Orchards' silver blossoms with fields of smoke.

Rivers of Night

Tonight must vex this troubled soul with dreams
Of swords and helmets black against cold stars,
Inexplicable armies, futile wars.
Faces recur with long forgotten names,
Forsaken lovers, half extinguished flames.
Daffodils must nod in the wind that roars
And calls to life past crimes and probes deep sores,
And bow their golden heads against the streams
Of rain rushing from far behind the sun,
Banners of wrongs performed and right undone.
They shake their golden bells against the storm.
Empty clothes arise out of earth and form
Implacable assemblies. Light has gone.
None can ride these rivers but I alone.

The Burning Bowl

Shelves in a cupboard; saucers, glasses, plates,
Morning's mundane tasks, light through a window,
Agony none can comprehend or know,
Rising like a storm that devastates
Hills and highways. Who has not suffered fate's
Implacabilities or heaven's slow
And patient judgment? Memories that glow
Unexpected, unsought. Time penetrates
The heart like sudden daybreak out of black
And brilliant cloud that blazes forth, falls back
Into its angry dark. The burning bowl,
White cup that gleams and scarifies the whole
Cascading, laughing world, the mind arrayed
For peace and battle, dazzled, undismayed.

The Mind

What can you draw out of a damaged mind?
Its moods are roughly severed, twitching, burned
And ravaged limbs, and it bears raw scars, earned
In failure and tyrannies of the blind,
Errors of self and others, all unkind,
Remembrances of deep love not returned,
Cold gulfs of loss. But there is something learned,
That death and happiness are intertwined,
That being cannot be without pure thought,
And reason is the trace of God who wrought
The tall pine, the grey stone, flowering hill,
Made living spirits free to choose at will,
To listen courteously, to know the force
Of friendship, and the daybreak of remorse.

The Life-Raft

Caught in the drifting whirlpool of the mind,
An icy storm where scraps of shipwrecks flew,
Spun, vanished, I could not surface to view
The pastures where cattle and horses find
Nutritious crops blown by the golden wind.
Or, floundering in a rip tide that drew
Souls far from beaches into churning, blue,
Departed ocean, desperate, maligned,
Haunted by jellyfish and sharks that stared,
I was the unremembered, unprepared,
Struggling from devastation to dismay,
Until the Lord on quiet wings of day
Brought reason's life-raft and the bloodstained cross,
Water, forgiveness and redemptive loss.

The Droplet and the Sea

They come to mind, the failures, every scar
Given to self and others. Then blood streams
On shadowed rocks, and through the darkness gleams
The red trace of fatalities of war.
Did I summon them? No. They wake to mar
Tranquillity and unassuming dreams
With sudden nightmare, half-remembered themes
Arriving uninvited from afar,
Or closer than the droplet to the sea
That surges, tosses, roars incessantly,
Wrestles with its beaches and warm bays,
Deep tides and sandy ripples, lifts and sprays
The wind with salt and mist. From it arose
Consciousness, heaven's rapture, death's repose.

Air from Heaven

Reason recoils in dread, declines to trace
Histories and lineaments of old
Wrecks, failures and mortifications, rolled,
Swept, drifting on the surf of days, the race
Of winds and waves. This is the heart's disgrace,
Never to know itself, nor once unfold
The tangled weeds, the miry currents, cold
And half-remembered loss. Love can displace
All error and confusion. Love makes new
Syllogisms of kindness and forms true
Streams of daylight that gather on the wind,
As sunflowers reach for the warmth and find
Morning's refreshment and the soft sky's breath,
And air from heaven lifts the soul from death.

The Mourner

After the calamity, when your soul
Staggers, cracked and bleeding, from a new dawn
To a cold nightfall, neither mind nor brawn
Will struggle past the trivial daily roll
Of meeting rooms, reports and conflicts whole,
Uninjured. Gates of ivory and horn
Pour forth phantoms, visions, nightmares born
From long estrangement. Then what can console
The mourner? There is light beyond the day.
It wells and flows above the timid, grey
Shadows of twilight flecked with cloud, and brings
Promise of strange adventures, reckonings,
New friendship, songs that no thought can conceive,
Wordless and silent hymns to those who grieve.

The Thief

An hour came when I wondered if I could
Avoid all marks and imagery of grief,
All that awakens memory, the thief
Of work and calm and what remains of good
After hard wars and injuries withstood,
Immortal weapons glowing past belief,
Guns laid down for temporary relief,
And only temporary, from the flood
Of ruin, fire and sadness. Then I saw
There's no escape from nature's holy law
And all things must be known. I could not ask
Friends, workmates to exempt me from my task,
Speak only mundane words, for there are none,
And all things carry scars under the sun.

VI. The Mounting Tide

The Wounds of Faith

Faith

Could I select a glass to contemplate
The nightmare of the past etched in my face,
I would not choose one, no, not though its case
Were platinum, pearl, gold or silver plate,
Had I to gaze into it at the state
The centuries have brought me to, the trace
Of wreckage. Not mine only the disgrace,
But far, accusing generations wait
To name the mercenaries of the world.
And I remark myself in all the old,
The young, the gentle, strident and the child.
And I perceive myself also defiled,
As all are, by stained morning, muddled night,
Visions of death, with faith to rise and fight.

The Choice

I thought to grasp freedom and rest from what
Consumed me, hour by moment, street by block,
The consciousness of loss, the daily shock
Of all that could have been, all that was not.
I plunged myself in flame and ice and hot
Indulgence, as if strange flesh were a rock.
But none may choose to sink back to the stock
Of dull, brute animals who once has thought
And known. All may find heaven's living walls
As angels, or endure sequential falls
Far lower than the unoffending sheep
Or cattle that browse, reproduce and sleep,
Than dancing butterflies and fertile beasts,
Crimson, wailing parrot or wolf that feasts.

Gate of Emptiness

Time expands, contracts, and reveals its great
Perplexity of movement, change, display
Of what was, what could not be, and what may
Not live again. Time's angry lions wait,
Glowing like cold, white mornings, at the gate
Of emptiness and fire. Trails of smoke stray
Outward from grim remains of yesterday,
Ghosts of tomorrow, thoughts that came too late
For action or completion, dreams that stand
As monuments to enterprise ill planned,
Carried out badly, shadows of dull pain,
Monuments that diminish in the rain
And dusk of history, or hopes that spring
To grace and life when dawn comes glistening.

Hours of Emptiness

They come in hours of emptiness and light
That fades and softens into gentle grey,
Then deeper grey, then black; that falls away,
And shadows grow and spread, extend their height
And wrap the world in secrecy and night.
Distraction ebbs and reason ends its play,
And age-old images wander and stray,
Break into sudden flame in thought's despite.
They come, the deaths that passed decades ago,
Questions whose answers none may ever know,
Histories of wreckage and disdain,
Stones crumbling in long wind and sun and rain.
Not time itself can change time that has been,
And days once seen can never be unseen.

The Bridge

To find out what it means to be broken –
There is an education for the soul.
A school for which only the lost enrol
And learn their cherished loves were mistaken,
Feel bones and sinews, mind, reason shaken,
Premises from conclusion, part from whole,
Cartilage from tendon. To pay the toll
And find the road is wrecked, the bridge fallen,
Bitumen and concrete in the river
With rusted cars abandoned forever.
Now I must learn to travel and go where
True propositions flourish in clean air,
Find freshly planted fields growing, and sun
Rising into its flames when night is done.

Spirit's Dawning

That is not love that counts convenience,
That seeks its own good at another's cost,
Its own salvation though another's lost,
That uses and discards its instruments,
Revokes its choices for expedience
And turns, when whom it claimed to love is crossed
By frailty or misfortune, into frost.
That is not love that studies requirements.
And on the round, impassioned, teeming earth,
Love is the freshly breathing body's birth,
The spirit's dawning. Love will not decide
To hunt for self in hopelessness and pride.
Love is more constant than the wind that blows,
The rain that feeds the grapevine and the rose.

Forgotten Hills

To feel the passions and the dreams that linger,
So it is to walk among steep, high, cold
Pines that toss a shrill wind with lives untold
Or spoken only to the soil, the litter
Of cones and dropped branches. Or to wander
On beaches by strange seas where waves have rolled
Through endless years and rumbled in their old
Confusion and green turbulence forever,
Labour on brutal streets and witness in
A wounded passer-by dullness of sin,
Inexpugnable joy and hidden peace.
To learn how pride and ignorance may cease,
To watch white, faint stars fade when cool suns break
On grey, forgotten hills, and young worlds wake.

The Mounting Tide

One scorching noon I walked to the far end
Of a battered, grey, long, wooden jetty,
Faded under decades of high, empty
Sunlight welling down from bare sky; chastened
By slow seasons of rain and pounding wind.
I stood and watched the sea's lift, the salty
Waves and ripples blending in their mighty
Turbulence and tumult away from land.
Gazing outward and forward from the brink,
I pondered how stray wreaths of seaweed sink
And break to fragments in the mounting tide,
And thought how much I thought I knew had died,
Vanished like shoals of passing sand that flow,
Disperse and dwindle while deep currents grow.

The Moonflower

All things murmur the joy of being true.
Bright branch, pale water, raven's acrid song,
The rhythm of a horse's mane, the strong
Hunger of hunting dogs. The cockatoo,
Red-tailed, brilliant black, light playing through
Dark, netted leaves, the day's declining, long
Fade to chill night and the first stars among
Dispersing clouds and air that cools from blue
To soft marine and into twilight sky.
And I could speak the truth or I could lie,
Choose to welcome or not the parrot's wail,
The lake's eddy. Hopes and families fail,
And truth is in the moonflower, the grass,
The newborn child, though unseen ages pass.

The Vow

Everything must crumble, sooner or now.
We are not what we were nor shall be yet.
The felled tree shows its rings, does not forget
That once it towered over field and plough,
Resisting angry storms that fought to bow,
And maddened rain to drown it. None may let
Past years rush over him without regret
Or changeless memories. Therefore I vow
To set aside antagonism, and judge
Few but myself, nor feed a sterile grudge,
Nor dull resentment. This oath too I break,
Twist rhyme and reason, set my thought to shake
Fixities of the past, fail to erase
The barren destinies, the shame of days.

VII. A Vine Dances

Hades

"Fallen," I said, "the cruel king is fallen."
Arrows and firebrands scattered in their pride
A thousand feet below the crumbled side
Of rocky pastures on a steep mountain.
Giant limbs and weapons, severed, broken
On sheared pines, lay spread out rough and wide
Among the scree; ended infanticide,
Golden blades and sacrifice of children.
I watched him slip, sway, curse and tower high,
Slither on battered stone, fall, grasp the sky.
His bloodstained axe dropped, shattered, among sparse
Pine needles and rare, thin, disordered grass.
A thousand graceless armies called to be
Ten thousand lords of Hades worse than he.

The Waking Stars

Griefs that fell far, too far away for word,
For music, rhyme, or song or symphony,
Resolve themselves into the storm, the sea,
Dark, lumbering, high clouds, gold sunlight, blurred
And breaking in its brightness on waves stirred,
Compounded, gathered, flung, enchained, set free
By endless tides, cold winds, the tyranny
Ancestral ocean's living laws conferred
On this unchanging moment. Griefs that dream
Beneath the tremor of the hand, the gleam
That sees afternoon sink into the bay,
Transform themselves to tears for ending day,
Reveal the waking stars, the dawn of night,
The secret riddle, grey sleep of twilight.

A Vine Dances

Visions of vanished love, fragile and white,
Flicker like burning arrows in the bare
Summits of trees, illuminating air,
Wind and starting raindrops. Elusive, slight,
Ungraspable, they flash and pass from sight,
Return and bring cold flame to high boughs where
Memories of forgotten beauty flare
And shine across the borders of the night,
So that an acorn lives, a fern frond glows,
A vine dances and hidden wonder grows.
Lights wake like silent streams that bend and fall.
Histories and prognostications call
The thoughtful eye to glimpse love that shall be,
Playing forever, terrible and free.

The Hidden Rose

Doors open and multifaceted song
Pours without sound over the wide stone stair
Down from a terraced building, fills warm air,
Purifies the darkening road, the long
Lines of cars asleep, the shadowy, strong,
Sheltering trees. Intangible and rare,
Unseen, unheard, but more securely there
Than all the past cacophonies of wrong,
Confusions, lies, bewilderments, it grows
While twilight fades, touches the hidden rose,
Brushes the curved, black railing with its notes,
A panoply of melodies that floats
In weaving, dancing staves no sight can sense,
Transfigures dusk's fear, evening's violence.

The Library

Austere, immutable, alive and free,
Rippling with gleams of laughter and delight,
The harmonies of day and songs of night,
The mischief of a well-formed comedy,
Time and impassioned truth in tragedy,
Philosophical wisdom in despite
Of mounting errors and the mornings' flight,
Such and all others is the library,
Shelves in their ranks and files reaching to bare
And neutral ceilings in conditioned air,
Burdened by learning and mistakes that wait
For fresh arrivals to investigate
Implacable geometries of breath
And spirit, riddles of despair and faith.

Mind's Fire

A book with tattered pages, damaged spine,
Its author's name all but illegible
From years' clumsy handling, disrespectful
Storage in all weathers, fog and sunshine,
Might yet convey strong meaning, line by line,
Leaf by smudged leaf, mind's fire in potential,
Whether one pause to read it, or the dull
Stranger cast it aside for the malign
Deliverances of the shining screen,
A messenger from ages lost as green
Grasses replaced by concrete, rust, despair,
Or a soft breath of unpolluted air,
Terror, unreason, hatred or the warm
Song of deep rationality, true form.

The Rose

To take measure of a lifetime's wrongness,
An evening's passion or a summer day
That cannot be recalled or thought away,
Nor its slow, entangled consequences;
Beliefs drawn from an era, from distress
Of television, paper, film, song, play
That lost worlds praise and so are held astray;
To have refused the greater, loved the less;
Who may stand back from sorrow and an age,
Rewrite the tattered, half remembered page?
Only I learn to suffer and repent
Of every morning wasted, night misspent,
Perceive the dawn sun in all hearts that ache,
Revere the rose that flowers, boughs that break.

The Scales

I am weighed in the scales and found wanting.
So it seemed, and so it was, when some chance
Called back an agonizing circumstance,
Sunlight on gentle green roseleaves flowing,
A white cloth in a restaurant glowing,
A kiss, a night of flame, a spurious glance
Of love that changed too soon to the slow dance
Of denigration. A dry creek panting
For rain that would not fall. The hard grey sand
Swirling over a rolling, ancient land.
Ripe water plays. Gold nasturtiums flourish.
Flowers bring truths and your fresh grapes nourish.
Judge not lest you be judged, the great words say.
You gathered herbs and threw the scales away.

Tides of Daybreak

The tides of daybreak meet the surging dream
Of ecstasy and tumult and the quaint
Artefacts of murderer, fool and saint
Arrayed in sculpted ranks by time's cool stream.
Images of impossible stars gleam,
Faltering one by one and growing faint
Before the rising rays of dawn that paint
Blank walls and faceless homes with gold, and seem
Just for a moment's promise to give heart
To thoughts and visions years have torn apart,
Scattered on the hollow bank like driftwood
Statues of the morning, as if light could
Remove the heavy fog of night's long dread,
The river's rubble and the ghosts who fled.

The Fountain

Love is a fountain constantly flowing,
A surge of water that answers the high,
Quick, changeable, companionable sky,
Shivers and dances in summer's growing
Heat and winter mountains' piercing, snowing
Summits and slopes, a flood that ponders why
It comes to flourish, pause and rest and die
And run again, rises from long knowing,
Deep clefts of suffering and buried walls,
Cold caverns of secrecy, waterfalls
Glimmering under limestone, shafts of light
Echoing from the soaring rainclouds' height,
Breaks hearts and worlds, or serves the humble truth
That streams like rain through all the tortured earth.

VIII. Sanctities of Dawn

The Wounds of Faith

The Shivering Flame

There is a constant one who speaks to me,
And has done always, though I would not hear,
And though I shrugged and sighed and followed mere
Shadows and wisps of joy's immensity.
More than the mind can think, or flesh can see,
The tide of being rises and draws near,
The heart is humbled, gathered into sheer
Silence, undying light and unity.
Then how to speak of self where self is none,
Of ending where new life plays in the sun?
Thought falters, meets its ground, returns to know
That every blade of grass must breathe and grow
Despite the winds of darkness and of blame,
And each soul is its own shivering flame.

Orchards

All shall know themselves in every other,
See how the vision of the land that's theirs,
Deep orchards red with apples, pale with pears,
White and pink cherry blossoms that flutter
Affectionately in the wind's whisper,
Is given to the passing soul that cares
To pause and view transcendency and shares
Trees, harvest, family. Sister, brother,
Parent and child shall learn how all things done
In cruelty or love to anyone
Are shown to me. And whatever I give
To break peace or to help a stranger live
Is offered to myself, and heaven's light
Flowers and sings, though flames consume the night.

Seeds of Kindness

There but for the grace of Christ, the fires
That burn and scar, consume, displace, renew,
Heat dull, brown, twisted iron into blue
Steel blazing louder than the cold stars' choirs;
But for unending mercy that requires
Only acceptance of slow seasons, new
Foliage when fresh sunlight pouring through
Tangled boughs onto the rough stream inspires
Harmony, love, freedom; but for a flood
Of wind and rain to wash away thick mud
And fill the fields with sudden, rising, white
And gold flowers, ephemeral and bright;
There, like an erring dreamer, I would go,
But for the seeds of kindness, winds that blow.

Dawn

Flowers ripple on a green hedge. Their blue,
Soft petals dance. Fresh butterflies take wing,
Fragile, golden, rapid. Wasps whirl and sting.
Dawn's gentle waking summons morning dew.
In years of childhood everything is new.
Dark rain and sudden storms patter and sing.
Wonder does not cease or ebb with passing
Seasons and age, but deepens, proves more true
How I am here and free, more clear and right
When trees waltz in the wind, or where a height
Of tumbled mountains clambers to the sky,
And others are as light and whole as I,
Now love survives and conquers midnight's wars,
And grapevines grow towards the dwindling stars.

Shadows of Ecstasy

I am no longer I, but something draws
Footsteps, thoughts, onward, backward and around
Shadows of ecstasy and far, profound
Images of the world's eternal laws,
Painted in dry, shed blood, carved by rough claws
And memories of ruin. Rugged ground,
Branches and winds that whisper truth surround
The faith that grows and flowers without pause
Through the morning and evening, winter's cold
And summer's warm, unquenchable, fierce gold.
What then, or who, can this be that displays
Still riper, richer fields through hours and days?
And now I am more truly I, when night
Reveals high stars and thought dissolves in light.

Sanctities of Dawn

When ruin is completed, something stirs,
Murmur of light, a breath among the reeds,
Crops that will sprout from once discarded seeds,
A highway pitted by past travellers,
Orchards of long forgotten gardeners.
Death becomes the returning life that feeds.
Barrenness ends, fertility succeeds.
Quiet music summons the harvesters.
Green wheat flourishes and cool streams flow
Between stone houses broken long ago.
The wind does not forget a city lay
Where now it rises, whirls and falls away,
Plays with the roses, cools the raging thorn,
Calls midnight into sanctities of dawn.

Mists

The dawning breath of consciousness; a crow
Pushing its head forward, lifting its beak
To wail; a laughing child who learns to speak;
Emotion's deep descents, logic's cool flow;
A soldier's quiet agony; the slow
Chant of an individual, unique
Through all blind time and entropy can wreak;
The passion and the gentleness to know.
Christ beckons out of mists and chance and fire
Selves born to think, live, suffer and inspire,
Eyes formed to close in placid sleep and wake
To watch the soft winds turn, the morning break.
These are the vivid signs that touch the soul.
Earth, bones and ash find truth, hearts become whole.

The Land Set Free

The sky secludes itself and worlds retreat.
The burdened mind withdraws into dull shade.
Neglected homes and waiting bushes fade.
Confusion masks the pavement and the street,
Darkens each living creature that I meet,
Until at last the land appears, displayed,
Set free by that same kindly lord who made
And forms all things afresh with every beat
And breath of time that none can comprehend,
So that new daisies glow and grasses bend,
Water ebbs and rises and strange sunlight
Flames on high boughs under the mounting night
Of clouds' darkness. Trees dance. The mind returns
To presence and the fire of pardon burns.

The Cliff

animula, vagula, blandula – Hadrian

Poor, ungraspable, naked, fearful soul,
It fleets like rays of light from a sunrise
That fills the fields with music and the skies
With pink and cold red flame; flies to its goal
Through meeting room and office, plays its role
Of shameful pragmatism, feels the surprise
Of truth that breaks like lightning on dazed eyes,
Cascading, sudden, springing out as whole,
Living illumination, soaring down
To darkness. Then harsh rain scourges the town,
And hailstones batter cars. The soul must cry
Its name like wind that thrills down from a high
Cliff to tremble around the fallen stone,
Know failure, pass to other hills, alone.

Faithful Joy

What am I but a wanderer who feeds
On flesh and lust and water, crusts of bread,
Ambition, wine, sleep, anger and the dead,
A creature of the dawn that fights and bleeds,
Pursues a fantasy that still recedes
In fog and clamour? Ignorant, ill-read,
Prey to sharp winds that fill an empty head,
Servant of opinion. Christ intercedes,
Provides the precious chance to save a child,
Cleanses the wounds time's madness has defiled,
Offers the thought of friendship and the gifts
Of love and faithful joy, a song that lifts,
Sunlight that shelters vine leaves on a wall,
Unforeseen plants that follow soft rainfall.

IX. Immortalities

The Wounds of Faith

Immortalities

Something leaps and whispers, wanders and twists,
Uncertain, tenuous, through walls of cloud,
Battlements of rain, and when the proud,
Incessant sun consumes the land; makes fists
At morning and evening. Something persists,
Indomitable, frightened, when the loud,
Vigorous cries of its accusers crowd
Calamitously close by. It resists
Determinism, atoms' compulsion; flees
The hard, bare cliffs, love's immortalities,
To find them looming in the roads of night,
Or constant in the warm, peaceful twilight.
Only one law constrains its path: it must
Live and live on when all the stars are dust.

King of Fire

What calls a chastened, haunted animal
Out of its covert in the frozen clay,
Trailing fragments of earth, red blood and grey,
Departed leaves? King of the terrible
Firestorm, arbitrator of the battle
Between grass and wind, master of the play
Of burning instants on the changeless way
From creation to ash, the festival
Of freedom, choice, conscience and love that breaks
The spirit and the dream while hunger shakes
Perception into dust, why will you send
This fragile self on rescues without end,
To succour children, brides and starving dogs,
Nurse its flickering light through mists and fogs?

Silences

Lord of the windstorm and the cyclone's wail,
Whistling, spreading wreckage over the fields,
Yours is the murmur of quiet that shields
The fragile spirit in the ruthless gale,
The gentle breezes billowing the sail,
The sighing, shimmering water that yields
Gracefully when a suffering hand wields
A swaying craft. Night shivers and grows pale.
Darkness fades like dawn frost and melts away.
Yours is the silence of the glowing ray
Approaching its new home. When the deep storm
Plummets into terror, still then you form
The mercy of the silences. A sound,
Unheard, unanswered, touches holy ground.

Calming the Tides

Can he that told the woman at the well
Of all her life, her husbands and her friend,
Whose voice could calm rough tides and reprehend
Tumultuous waves and menacing high swell,
Had witnessed long past ages, could foretell
The temple's ruin, history's last end,
Give the blind new visions of light, or mend
Limbs that had never walked, whose words dispel
Shadows of infamy, who suffered death,
Can he not name and number every breath
Of love or cowardice, contempt, disdain,
Measure the morning dream of guilt or pain,
Counsel the ravaged heart, the surging will,
The mind's inconstant currents to be still?

The Fleeting Land

Remoter than the furthest galaxy,
Burning, silent, billions of years apart,
Stranger than an astrophysicist's art
To name and quantify stars' history,
Logical to wreck the philosophy
That lowers beauty to the fit and start
Of neutrons, closer than the beating heart
In the late hours when sleep declines our plea,
Elusive as a rainbow's many shades
When daylight sinks behind a cloud and fades,
Grass flickers in the last sun, or a thought,
A memory escaped as soon as caught,
Immediate as love the secret hand
That shapes earth, sky, breath, rain and fleeting land.

The Wounds of Faith

The Mirror and the Tree

From the highest crag on cliffs of grey stone,
Concentrating fierce light above wild sea
Whose white, spreading waves roll implacably,
Foaming on long, brown sand and then are drawn
Back into green tides that clamour and moan,
And were before the mirror and the tree,
And shall outlast all human history,
From that far peak down to the secret zone
Where lust and anger lie below the mind,
Nursing their vengeances, their shameful, blind
Futilities, there is that one who knows
And nourishes each living soul that grows,
Kindles the sun flaring above the sky,
And hears the ruthless, grieving ocean's cry.

The Sighs of Time

Immortal spirit, born in blood and rain,
Measured and weighed by timeless, burning lights,
Young offspring of an ephemeral night's
Eternal ecstasy, soul born through pain,
Awaking in new majesty to gain
Rhythms of breath and vision's dawning flights,
Embarked upon a voyage of delights,
The passion of awareness and the stain
Of suffering and ignorance, the gift
Given in joy and mercy of the lift
Of flowers on a supple morning breeze,
A loving hand, the twilight's majesties,
You shall outlive the suns, the sighs of time,
Flourish beyond the worlds, entire, sublime.

The Window

Every road and valley is a window
That opens on a daily mystery,
Nocturnal measures of identity,
Mountains, high boughs, fallen branches that flow
On white rivers down to wide fields. They glow,
Grey twig, dark stone, leaf's waving destiny,
Presence of individuality,
Drifting, eternal, true, changeless, although
A million million centuries should pass.
A breath of wind or fragile blade of grass
Reveals a suddenness, uncovers new
Redemption in a purple flower, blue,
Sharp, silver blossoms, dedicated faith,
Cool water's joy, contingencies of earth.

The Sun Awakes

Mornings break unrecognised that prepare
Catastrophes and endings. Dancers call,
Sing for an audience that endures all
The dawn of tragedy, lightening air,
Labours to sympathise, to reason, care,
Suffers the story's windings. The seeds fall
Where they will. Crops of golden wheat grow tall.
Bright poison berries clamber over bare
Granite cliffs. The sun awakes to see
Unguessable beginnings, comedy
Changing to scenes of blood, revenge, and cold
Conspiracies that break the heart and fold
Noon into twilight. None can tell whose lives
Flourish or stumble before night arrives.

The Sea's Amazement

Bewildered souls dare unmeasured ocean,
Rocks of random events, disordered thought,
Treacherous, delusive currents, are caught
By backward tides that gather depths and run
From evening down to morning, and from sun
To moon and stars over a sleeping port,
A harbour lapped by leaping waves that sport
Inconsequently through long confusion,
Gleaming, black, irresolute, until
A secret light begins to grow and fill
The sea's amazement with new sanctity.
Undying spirit finds its destiny
To look upon the rolling shore, the coast,
The breath of life, the sky's returning host.

X. Gatherer of Days

The Wounds of Faith

Absolution

It is forgiven. Forests drown in long,
Tumultuous clouds, falls and gusts of high,
Sweeping rain. Grey sand melts under the sky.
Its fragments dance. And all the cruel wrong
That weights earth is a note in joy's deep song,
A moment's disharmony, or a dry
Leaf before the storm, a bird's lonely cry
Before the sea comes in to still its tongue.
Mine and yours, even our darkening age
Of dead philosophy, our heritage
Of smallness, meanness, agonising loss,
Innocence torn again upon the cross,
Burning forests flooded by the ocean,
Quenched and purified. It is forgiven.

Gatherer of Days

All ages past appear in ranks of gold,
Silent, measured columns, impassive halls
Arriving from the clouds. The trumpet calls
And histories return and truths unfold
Their certainty and loss. Hours never told
Reveal themselves impartially on walls,
Carved, sculpted marble rising into falls
Of sunlight, shafts of mist, echoes from old,
Relinquished centuries. Concealed too long,
Steep galleries appear of vivid wrong
And intricately patterned victory.
Gatherer of days out of imagery,
He lifts his arms above the sculpted flight,
Bearing the faithful storm, the wells of light.

Cloud of Mystery

The rose, the sunbeam, remote worlds that bleed
Light across the boundaries of the sea,
The memory of evening, a pine tree
Gathering its dark fire, a lone, stray weed
Straggling over grey sand. All things proceed
From silence and potentiality,
Arise to the brief actual. To be
Is only to be caught in storm and reed,
Cold sunrise, mounting nightfall, and to share
Growth and diminution, to find the rare
Chance to remember how the flood that pours
Reveals the trace of heaven that endures.
Rose, rain and shore emerge out of a cloud
Of mystery to play and sing aloud.

The Sculptor

He will shape and break hearts as a sculptor
Whose patient fingers move the stubborn clay
Into new grace when streaming shafts of day
Fill the studio with light and vigour,
Work with skilful vision to transfigure
A heavy mass into the moving play
Of limbs and features; as an artist may,
Who strikes and torments marble with hammer
And chisel, battering resistant rock
With judged, measured carving and sudden shock,
Revealing out of crude and errant stone
Something unimaginable, unknown,
Unheard, before the hands of heaven bring
The changed, impassioned soul to walk and sing.

Islands

This is the strangest of all things, most true
And inexplicable, that here should be
Molecules whirling from infinity,
From silence into silence, to renew
The restless morning of the leaping, blue
And always changing power of the sea.
That these currents today should form the three
Low, rocky islands no one may undo,
Geology cast now into the stream
Of endlessness where living spirits gleam,
The music of the lumbering waves' roar,
Unrepeatable foam racing ashore.
Above the beach a golden, dancing stand
Of trees, black seaweed sleeping on white sand.

Moments of Light

Gather the findings of an intellect,
Gossamer threads dispersed in morning air,
Held for an instant in the sun's rough glare,
And soon ungraspable, invisible. Collect
Moments of light and save them from neglect,
Soft pools of silence, intricate and rare
Amid cacophonies and buses' blare,
A single flower in a desert, flecked
With sand, earth, wind; subtle reason's treasure
Tarnished by noise of work and loud leisure.
A fine stream falling from the highest cast
Of rock runs onward, makes its way at last
Into the secret, waiting, tidal flow,
Richer and more present than soul could know.

The Day

In the silent humility of prayer,
When mind and pulse confront the tide that flows
Through ashes, flame and dust-motes, and compose
Obeisances of consciousness that dare
The waters of the truth, spirit laid bare
In all its foolishness awakes and knows
How little good it brings, how much it owes
Time, freedom and creation. You are there,
Your quince tree growing up towards the light,
Rich love, green grapevines, bolls of cotton, white
And soft amid their dark, unfolding leaves.
My heart gives thanks for all that it receives,
Having endured the summers of dismay.
Apples and almond shoots embrace the day.

Before the Sun

Clothed in flesh like angels in their glory,
Golden, streaming hair, warm truths, pure kindness,
Eyes of sympathy; subject to distress
Of dissolution, illness, injury,
As all are; made to know and to be free;
A spirit, yours, in more than earthly dress
Comes with hope and visions of love to bless.
Vindication of the transitory,
As when a walker rounds a stony hill
Painted with grey lichen, grasses that spill,
Growth and green joy, and meets a swaying fall,
Many-coloured flowers, ephemeral,
Dancing, flowing, eternal as the light
Before the sun that calls them into sight.

Marigolds

Here is a riddle none can solve, a scroll
Only he that shaped it can decipher,
Enigmas of the half-revealed answer
Coded in the sun and seasons that roll
From dawn to sunset, east to west, from pole
To northern pole, and in shrubs that flower,
Cryptograms in moons that burn and shiver:
That one can love another living soul,
Find a spirit among billions, worth
All aching memories and mines of earth,
Embrace warm flesh and draw light from new thought,
Observe red marigolds and gifts unsought,
Unique light of each morning and the ways
Chosen companions welcome ends of days.

Miracles

Nights fall and mornings rise with miracles
No physics may describe. Though God should raise
To life the dead and cancel the decays
Of days or of millennia, though he calls
Wine from water and the high tempest falls
At his command to a light breeze that strays
Over the sea, a man disabled plays,
Runs, leaps and dances, yet the pinnacles
Of wonder come each hour a living soul
Awakens in a mother's womb to whole
And true selfhood, unique though galaxies
Blaze and fade, mountains crash into cold seas,
Lost armies form and conquer, cities rise,
End, burn, and the world opens to new eyes.

XI. The Feather

The Wounds of Faith

The Song

"It is not I," the weary worker said,
After a morning with a drunken thief
Who sought sobriety and chose relief
From anguished generations of the dead
That wrecked her mind and twisted it, and fed
Her moods with sullen anger, so that brief
Moments of happiness were also grief,
"It is not I who serve but something read
And written long ago, a breath that sighs,
A murmur above black, thundering skies,
Music that steers the sculptor's eye that makes,
And fills the singer's heart until it breaks,
The song that guided Leonardo's arm,
And moves my lips and hands to proffer calm."

Hand of God

The bestial, angelic and the child:
The camel snorts and wallows in its stall,
Hyenas scavenge, reproduce, and all
The innocent creation of the wild
Pursues returning nights, never reviled
By history or guilt, impossible
Regrets or dreams. Only this animal
Whose instincts war with mind, unreconciled,
May know the grim disturbances of thought,
The comfort of the word, the battles fought
Between the brute beast's hunger, fear and sloth,
Angel's patient intellect, infant's growth,
The reeking dung of fifty thousand sties,
The hand of God who lifts faith to the skies.

The Veil

The more I mount the steep hills and admire
The wave of wind, the polished granite's blaze,
Far slopes and valleys fading into haze,
The whirring insects' intermittent choir,
The focussed sun's individual fire,
Or wander by a cool, dark river's ways,
Sheltered by trees that bend to drink, and raise
Their dense and varied leaves, the more entire
The certainty that all things are a veil,
Ephemeral, uncountable and frail,
Before the gentle lord who made and gives
Eternal joy to all that is and lives.
More vivid, too, the passion of each stone,
The fall of clay, unchangeable, alone.

Love and Symmetry

At the first forming of the timeless stars,
It was ordained that spirits should be free
To watch the dawn and know their history,
Burn buildings and riot in brawls and jars,
Or comfort the bereaved and heal their scars
And speak true words of love and symmetry.
For none can think that has not liberty,
No mechanism gaze through iron bars
Of hard necessity to shape a tale,
Or paint dark ocean and a shining sail,
See characters and tragedies unfurled,
Or journey to the founding of the world,
Choose death, or labour to nourish a child
With food and joy and music undefiled.

Havens

Generations after generations
Laboured thousands of years with brick and clay,
With turbulence of thought, painting and play,
Reasonable, subtle explanations,
To shape homes, families, lay foundations
To shelter spirit from the storms of day.
Churches, houses not to be wrenched away
By war's blood-stained tides and lamentations,
Or by the barren leaders who would tear
Down memory and life, let freezing air
Pour over frightened children, and applaud
The wrecked and scattered statues of their flawed
And human forebears. They shall pass and fade.
Havens will flourish that true hands have made.

The Comet

The comet streaming flame above cold earth,
Trailing over dark sea its timely fire,
The nebula's enigmas and its dire
Clouds of consuming emptiness, the birth
Of constellations cannot pass in worth
The sound of a child starting to respire
In a small room, or a tree's golden spire
Lifting past scattered rock substantial breath
Of greenery and sunlight. No kind words
Of sympathy and truth, nor a grey bird's
Wings catching light in a black thunderstorm,
Shall lose the trumpets of their shining form
And chords of their exactness, nor the sun
Rising past shoals and reefs that dance and run.

Artisan

The mind takes flame and works its thoughts as gold
Softens and melts in a furnace and glows,
Dazzling a craftsman's shielded eyes. It flows,
Fierce and hot, towards its destined mould,
Assumes new form and harmony as rolled
And piled ingots, delicate rings, or rows
Of spears, knives, brooches. It submits and knows
Intricate majesty of fold on fold,
Shaped, subtle leaf. An image of a wing,
Flight without motion, tiny birds that sing
Harmoniously, silently, at rest,
And decorate a finger, throat or breast,
Catch light across a green courtyard, a blaze
Of sun's profusion or a soft eye's gaze.

The Glade

Here in this wide glade under arching trees,
Patches of deep shadow, peaceful sunshine
Stir, dance and tremble, echo the benign,
Soft shifts of high foliage in the breeze
That cools the sandy ground. Here is mind's ease,
Heart's healing under branches that combine
In changing music, wave and intertwine
And rustle gentle leaves. And history's
Ardours and ceaseless questionings proceed,
Break lives and cities, maim, devour and bleed
Bewildered populations. And you hear
The call of running water from a clear
Stream beyond the small wood. Ripples play,
Give refuge from barbarities of day.

The Golden Cave

Above the flailing tides, in grey sandstone,
Battered and worn by winds that swooped and fled,
A cave poured light forth, golden, purple, red,
Illuminating the harsh waves' pale moan,
The water's ways and looming currents, thrown
Together from far floods and reefs. It spread
New radiance over the ripples and shed
Its colours onto remote sands. Maroon
Flickers crossed the foam, and scarlet beams
Touched swirling pools and unremembered streams,
Gesturing over schools of fish. Bright rays
Brought unprecedented flame to small bays
And anchorages, reached down to the slow,
Green, unknown worlds where silent spirits grow.

The Feather

The wind soars, whistles in the distant height
Of trees whose shadowed branches toss and tear
Mountainous gulfs of sighing, whirling air,
The patched and starlit emptiness of night,
And creak and groan. The wind pursues its flight,
Wheels and plummets around an open, bare,
Relinquished field. It leaps on cold earth where
Scattered stray rocks appear. They touch the light
Breaking past harried clouds. A feather falls,
Glowing black, flickering red, through steep halls
Of turbulence; twists, pirouettes and slides.
Then, as an adept ballerina glides
And comes to rest on stage – her dark hair, crowned
With flame, subsides – it settles on grey ground.

XII. The Sleeping Sea

The Flame

A song rose in a wilderness of hail,
Unruly wind and rain that pounded old,
Intolerable earth. Slow thunder rolled,
Shuddered, and a small, desperate bird's wail
Wandered into the grey downpour. A frail,
Tenacious, grappling plant struggled to hold
Its thin roots in the sliding, battered, cold
Land white, sharp stones attacked. The far song's trail,
Unheard or all but unheard in the loud
And omnipresent roar of storm and shroud,
Played its eternal melody, its warm
And answerable words of peace and form,
An orchestrated flame, a burning path
Unquenched by thunder, ice or winter's wrath.

The Sleeping Sea

Near a forgetful town stands a high hill,
More placid than slow hymns, in the fierce light
From a hard sun, and garlanded with white,
Primrose, yellow, blue flowers, and marble
Caves veined with pale rock, silver, green, purple
And gold. Brilliant bushes trail from the height
Around the shining earth, dark stone, leaves bright,
Shiver and dance in the summer heat, until
They fall into red soil at the land's root,
Or reach towards the sun, or guard small fruit,
Cupping crimson berries in warm, gnarled palms.
Water trickles through deep clefts, pours cool arms
To greet a chanting, broad, peaceful river,
A soaring, hot sea that sleeps forever.

Night Sky

Living white stars played a silent fanfare,
Ancient music that none may understand,
Performed before the hills arose, the land
Appeared from untrammelled seas, or air
Arranged itself to nourish breathing, dare
Consciousness, new thought; above grey hills planned
From time's beginning instant; secret sand,
Millennial mountains; cold, still grass, a bare
Creek bed, pale boughs bending over the low
Channel where water streamed seasons ago;
Scars of fire; glinting, half-visible stone,
A dreaming townsite, houses lost, alone.
The sky sank down behind the rocks and slept.
The moon looked on the crumbling earth and wept.

The Coast

A shadowy, long, moonlit coast of sand,
Low, enigmatic hills obscured by night,
Ocean that breaks and whispers into white
Foam spreading and growing across the land,
A multiplying intricacy planned
And granted being far beyond the height
Of momentary centuries, the light
Falling on changing tides, drawn by the hand
That gives the body life and frees mind's thought
To roam forever past its anxious, fraught
And harried years, to study with the dead,
Or leave its prayers and hopes dismissed, unsaid,
To cherish tears and thankless memories,
Or know the gleaming waves, the burning seas.

Above the Cliff

Winds wail, bluster, bellow and beat the sea,
Batter the white and foaming surf, whirl sand,
Belabour lonely, bending trees. They stand
Among the low scrub and sigh helplessly,
Unheard under the howl of the salty
Blast buffeting torn atmosphere and land,
Tumult from the southern tides, the grand
Gales known and measured from eternity.
And here above the cliff we laugh and sway
And lean into the cold storm from the grey,
Rolling ocean. It leaps and springs and roars,
A messenger from harsh Antarctic shores,
Hurls mists and salt into the speckled caves
And carries gusts of rain on cloud-capped waves.

The Comforter

Through violence of death and the slow dream
Of ships' collisions in white seas of smoke,
Then looking on realities that broke
All things that promised freedom, still the stream
Of gentle truth persisted. The supreme
Test that days continued, and I woke
To long perplexities, could not revoke
The timeless ground of birds' calls, or the gleam
Of passing and eternal harmony.
An afternoon came when the changing sea
Caught ten thousand sunbeams, glimmered and burned.
The comforter who had not left returned.
Soft wings beat across a river mouth's wide
Calm, and ripples' inexhaustible glide.

Love's Logic

Reason groaned and languished in a fever.
Sea was fire, earth ice, and two could equal
Three, twelve or seventeen. The stars might fall,
Turn to rain and melt away forever.
Distances expanded without measure.
Time shrank to pinpricks. Mathematical
Terror joined hands with astronomical
Chaos. Grey, streaming rocks gleamed with fervour.
Truth was in the fields and the mind was numb.
Night waited for a lucid dawn to come.
It broke when least expected. Reaching west,
From eastern hills, grew light that truth had blessed,
Revealing where the scorned and injured lay,
And mercy called love's logic into day.

The Wounds of Faith

Ruined Beginnings

Death will ride in triumph, desperate kings
Caught at its chariot wheels, lords of the slow
Labour of civilisation brought low,
Their work derided. Ruined beginnings
Will burn in golden, scarlet fire and wings
Of flame that lift and fly to sunset's glow,
Ashen houses crumbling in the shallow
Dust of evening while the heron swings
Down from its post to feed in settling light.
And death will ride in triumph through the night,
Glorying over rubble. Seeds of blood,
Blood of martyrs, stronger than winter's flood,
Quiet words, unfashionable and true,
Will outlast death and grow and build anew.

The Child

A universe of living souls, a world
Of healing gardens lulled by quiet rain,
Memorials of ecstasy and pain,
Recovering from gusts and leaves that curled
Around low roofs, from battered winds that whirled,
Assailing dusty farms and hills in vain,
The town's paths, halls, motels and parks maintain
The destinies and changing lives, unfurled
And flowering, that redeem it from the cold.
Night roads of blazing stars could not unfold
The magnitude of splendour that awakes
With every careful step an infant takes,
This cooling afternoon, this passing day,
Along a green verge where soft shadows play.

The Stray Bird

Here at the summation of all it means
To live, and to be human, self-aware,
Bewildered by the daybreak and the glare
Of morning labours, here before waves' greens,
Their drifting shades, cold greys, the lost heart keens
And flutters like a stray bird far from where
Returning flocks disport in hostile air
Above new lands. It pines for welcome scenes,
Dawn's fresh chill over city, mountain peak.
But once known coasts, old houses, roads are bleak,
Familiar shores and long remembered eyes
Are strange and puzzling sequences of cries,
Compelling the proud soul to face the light
Falling as fire from heaven to steer its flight.

www.ingramcontent.com/pod-product-compliance
Lightning Source LLC
Chambersburg PA
CBHW072006290426
44109CB00018B/2152